Speak Greek E

36 easy phrases

to learn on the plane

By Jennie Kitching

By purchasing this book you agree that you have read and understand that all information is subject to the reader's interpretation. The authors will not be held accountable for any interpretations or decisions made by recipients based on information provided herein.

This information is for education and entertainment purposes only. All information and/or advice given to you herein should not take the place of any medical, legal or financial advice given to you by any qualified professional. Any names or characters within this book are the product of the author's imagination and any resemblance to real persons, living or dead is completely coincidental.

Disclaimer: No one can guarantee that you will be a success as this is up to you, which means you have the power within you right now to do the best you possibly can to be the best you can possibly be. It is my genuine intent that you benefit enormously from the information herein which is offered in good faith. In order to benefit from the information in this book you must put the information into action. Merely reading a book cannot do anything for you. The only way to determine how this information can help you to be successful is to examine each tip and use your own good sense to apply it in your own circumstances and evaluate your results.

Welcome Aboard!

This book is written by English folks who went on holiday to Greece and loved it so much, they stayed!

We have selected the easiest and most useful phrases for most situations you will encounter and presented them in an easy to follow lighthearted manner.

Read through the book sequentially to get the best out of it and to follow the connections within the text and make sure you have fun and speak what you see!

Author Biography

Jennie Kitching

Jennie just loves to make complex things easy! A teacher of The
Advanced Diploma in Hypnosis and A Master Hypnotist since 2003,
Jennie was awarded her first training qualification in 1994. Since that time
she has become a certified trainer of a variety of differing methodologies
in the corporate and private sector (including Louise Hay, '*You Can Heal
Your Life*', Susan Jeffers ('*Feel the Fear and Do It Anyway*'). Additional
study, notably of the works published by John Cleese and Robin
Skynner ('*Life and How to Survive It*)' enabled Jennie to incorporate the
more personal aspects of self-improvement into the traditional corporate
training arena (GKN, Dudley MBC, The Law Society, etc) designing and
delivering bespoke courses such as Pre-Retirement and Women's
Development. Jennie presents with humour and enthusiasm drawing on
this extensive knowledge base. Now she writes, teaches, continues her
private consultations and delivers this knowledge to as many people as
possible! You can contact her at info@hiprocom.com.

Jennie Kitching also has the accolade of being a GHR Accredited
Advanced Senior Hypnotherapist, one of only a few in the world and now
teaches others to that level.

She loves swimming underwater, plays the Ukulele and is an avid
Cosplay enthusiast.

This book is written by English folks who went on holiday to Greece and loved it so much, they stayed!

We have selected the easiest and most useful phrases for most situations you will encounter and presented them in an easy to follow lighthearted manner.

Read through the book sequentially to get the best out of it and to follow the connections within the text and make sure you have fun and speak what you see!

Acknowledgments and Dedication

With the greatest thanks to the lovely people of Greece (both Greek and English) and particularly of those Living in Rhodes together, for their contributions and enthusiasm in putting this short and fun work together.

Dedicated to all those who love Greece and her people and wish to improve communication between us all to enjoy our time in Greece more.

Thank you for reading!

Amazon reviews are really important to future writing projects for independent authors. Please leave a review for me because I would love to hear your thoughts about this book.

If you would like to receive your **FREE** preview of my next book please **email** info@hiprocom.com.

Thank you!

CONTENTS

AUTHOR BIOGRAPHY 4

THANK YOU FOR READING! 7

FOREWARD 10

1 DO YOU SPEAK ENGLISH – MILL LARTA ANGLIKA? 12

2 HELLO – YA! 14

3 YES – NE! NO – OCKY! 15

4 OKAY! – DAX! 16

5 I KNOW NOTHING! - ZAIRO TI PO TA! 17

6 GOOD – KALA! 18

7 GOOD MORNING, AFTERNOON, NIGHT – KALI MERA, SPERA, NICKTA 19

8 THANK YOU! – F HARRY'S TOE! 20

9 PLEASE, DON'T MENTION IT, YOU ARE WELCOME! –PARA KA LO! 21

10 WATER, NOW! – NERO, TORA! 23

11 BEER – BEERA! 24

12 WINE – KRA SEE! 25

13 BIG – MEGA LOW 27

14 SMALL – MIK REE 28

15 CHOCOLATE – SOKO LATA 29

16 ICE CREAM – PAGOT OH! 30

17 ANOTHER – ENNA ALLO 31

18 VEGETARIAN - HORTO FAGOS 32

19 TOILET – TWALETTA 33

20 TODAY, TOMORROW, ...34

YESTERDAY – SIMMERA, AVRIO, HECK TESS 34

21 HOW MUCH? – POSSO KARNY? 36

22 MONEY, FIVE TO FIFTY EUROS – LEFTA, PENDE TO PENINDER EUROS..37

23 WATCH OUT – PROSS SECARE..39

24 HELP – VOY EEETH IA..40

25 HERE &THERE – ETHOU & ECKY 41

26 STOP – STA MATTER..42

27 I'VE FINISHED – TELIOS, HAVE YOU FINISHED? – TELIO RASEE?..43

28 SALT – A LARTEA 44

29 CONTAINS NUTS? ALLERGIC! – KSIRI CARPI? ALLERG EKOS! 45

30 THIEF! – KLEFF TESS!..47

31 ARE YOU OKAY? - EEESA KALA? 48

32 CALL A DOCTOR - KAL EESE YATRO! 50

33 CALL POLICE! – KALESE ASTENOMIA 51

34 I AM LOST – EHO KATHY 52

35 I HAVE LOST MY PASSPORT – EKASSA TO THEA VATEERIO MO 53

36 CAR, BUS, AEROPLANE – AFF TOW KINNY, TOW, LEO FOR RIO, AERO PLANNO..54

THANK YOU FOR READING!..55

Foreward

Learning Greek - as daunting as it may sound - is not actually the gargantuan task we expect it to be. You actually speak quite a bit of Greek already, yet you do not know it – as many English words have Greek roots. So, you know NOTHING of the Greek language? Thank goodness, because this book is just for you.

In this book we have decided to show you how to speak Greek the easy way: the MEGA easy way in fact (that's Greek, by the way, 'mega'!) Just speak what you see and you'll get it in no time. Imagine how tricky it is to speak English when you think about it: 'no' is pronounced just like know and yet the metal 'lead' (led) sounds nothing like lead (leed) as in 'leading the way'. Did you read (reed) it or have you read (red) it? How can light become lit but fight can't become fit? If teachers have taught, have preachers praught? So let's firstly get off our high Alogo (horse) about daring to attempt to speak Greek in the first place and admit the English Language is pretty tricky too.

Greek is thought to be SO tricky to learn that the good news is nobody expects you to speak it expertly and just by giving it a go you will be hailed a hero! This book is not intended to teach you Greek well, though these simple and efficient phrases will get you going, and will probably bring about a few smiles too AND a free drink or two!

Now just before you think you may not be able to say a word of Greek, read on and amaze yourself.

Oh yes, please remember:

When you see a bold character in a word, that is where to put the emphasis. In Greek, emphasis is very important as you will find out from the first example.

All of the Greek words in this book are spelt phonetically not as they are actually spelt. It's easier this way.

Have fun!

1 Do you speak English – Mill Larta Anglika?

So, let's say you are blessed with dark locks and eyes, have a bit of a tan and like wearing jumpers in twenty degree heat; or maybe the security guard at the airport has had a particularly heavy night and is quite tired; you might be mistaken for Greek origin and be mistaken for a Greek person.

This is where it may be appropriate to say these immortal words to get them to switch to English and give you some relief.

Mill Larta Anglik**a** = 'do you speak English?'

As mentioned in the Foreward, it is important where the emphasis is in Greek as this phrase also means 'Speak English why don't you!' if you were to say it in command tone, with your voice going down at the end of the phrase.

So, a question is received as a question when your voice tone rises at the end. So if you don't want to demand your security guard speak English and would rather be awfully English and ask the polite question, then be careful to phrase this one as a question.

2 Hello – Ya!

You say hello sometimes, don't you? Though, that's a bit formal isn't it? I bet you say the word Hi more often, yes?   So, your first word is Ya, which is short for Yasas – Hello, Hi.

Y**a** = Hi. (Ya as in yak).

3 Yes – Ne! No – Ocky!

You know that we sometimes say, 'nah!' for 'no'? Well that could mean yes in Greek, depending on your accent. Ne, moreover, is the word for Yes, though be careful with that emphasis, noting the bold text. Now, you pronounce the 'e' as in 'Heck' this is easy!

Ne = Yes. (Ne as in neck).

You know that we sometimes say, 'okay' for 'yes'? Well that means no in Greek.

Ocky = No. (Like Hockey without the 'H')

So, have a practice now. Imagine someone wants you to buy something from them and you would really rather not, or perhaps you might be at a bar and your admirer does not seem to understand the English word for no, then it's time for a little Hockey, without the H. **O**CKY! Okay?

4 OKAY! – Dax!

Okay, okay, let's make it easy here.

When you shorten 'okay' (which is short enough, granted) you say, in your laconic manner KAY!

Well in Greek you say **D**AX! Got it? Okay?

Dax = Okay.

'Okay, Nothing!' I might hear you say in my imagination – which of course in Greek you will say as Dax, Ti Po Ta!

5 I Know NOTHING! - Zairo Ti Po Ta!

How much Greek do you already know? Zero? Kala! This is the book for you then! So you know as little as a ti in a pot, ah?   You'll hear this a lot, so good you know what it means.   Now you pronounce the 'a' as in the French 'Voila!' but that's another book.

Zairo = I know

T**i** Po ta! = Nothing. (Ti as in tip, Po as in pot, ta as in tar).

So, when an admirer comes up and says, Y**a**, offering you a choice of exotic drinks, are you going to say:

N**e** n**e** **D**ax.

Or

Ocky. T**i** Po ta! **D**ax?

---

6 Good – Kala!

Kala is a good word!   Really, it is good, it means good and it can be used for just about everything. I'm okay; it's okay; never mind as I can understand you can't speak Greek; thank you for your restaurant food order; you can through security now; yes your passport seems to be in order.

Kala = Good. (Kala as in calorie).

So now when someone offers you that free drink and you wish to express your enthusiasm, you can say,

Ya! Ne, Dax, Kala!   Hi, yes, okay, good!

7 Good Morning, Afternoon, Night – Kali Mera, Spera, Nickta

Kala, Kala, so now you know good. That's kala!

A whole new world opens up to you now as you can greet people anywhere at any time of day.

Dax, now you know that kala is good, well, kali is good too and so is kalo but let's not complicate things! English does not have gender differences for ashtrays and cars and the like and let's not concern ourselves with why morning, afternoon and night are feminine, they just are, Dax? Ne? Kala.

Kali Mera – Good morning

Kali Spera = Good afternoon

Kali Nickta = Good night.

8 Thank you! – F Harry's Toe!

Think of poor Harry and his toe. You might not be concerned, because you have worries of your own, but imagine our Harry having a poorly toe.

An uncompassionate person might say, 'Sod Harry's Toe!' or worse 'F Harry's Toe!' Well, there you are, you've just said thank you in Greek. Now you pronounce the 'o' as in the Spanish 'Ole' (Olay) but that's yet another book!

F Harry's Toe = Thank you. (Note that this phrase is said quickly).

9 Please, Don't Mention It, You are Welcome! –Para ka LO!

I like to think of this as a Pair of Culottes! A rather unfashionable, unuseful item of clothing, perhaps, this is one of the most useful phrases you can say in Greek because it covers so much ground!

What a brilliant phrase you can use for so many purposes. You can use it even to get somebody out of the way if you are trying to pass through a crowd as it is also excuse me. This means you can call the waiter over using it too. Brilliant. Kala, isn't it?

Para ka LO! Is a lovely word that Greek folks will say to you when you talk about F Harry's Toe and it will amuse you (honestly, it will) that whenever you say F Harry's Toe they seem to respond with offering you a pair of culottes.

It goes something like this, 'F Harry's Toe' … 'Para Ka LO!'

Para Ka L**O**! = Please/Don't mention it/You're Welcome/Excuse me!

10 Water, Now! – Nero, Tora!

Imagine that the infamous Roman Emperor, Nero, the guy who reportedly fiddled while Rome burned.

Well all that burning (fire is Foot-ya and yes, wouldn't your toes be hot in a fire?) required a great deal of water to put it out didn't it? So when you have that hot thirsty feeling in the beautiful Greek sunshine, remember Nero watching Rome burn and ask for Nero!

Nero = Water

Nero Para Ka LO! – Water please!

Tora = Now

So, if you want some water, tora, because you are really really thirsty, or your toes are on foot-ya, then this is the phrase for you:

Nero! Tora! – Water! Now!

11 Beer – Beera!

Ne. Dax. F Harry's Toe -Yes, okay, thank you.

I know you may fancy something a little stronger than Nero. So, how's about a Beer. Well, that's easy. And if you want to say, Beer please, well you know that too, here goes.

Beera, Para Ka LO! = Beer Please!

Beera = Beer

Then, when it comes, you say… come on, you know what to say now!

F Harry's Toe!

12 Wine – Kra See!

You want wine, are you crazy! Dax, okay. Ne, yes,
you can have wine too. Now the 'a' is pronounced as
in 'Ask for a drink in Greek'.

Wine is Kra see.

Kra See = Wine.

If you are particular about colour and you are cocky
enough to want red. Then:

Kok in O = red.

Kok in O Kra See, Para Ka LO. F Arry's Toe – Red
wine please. Thank you!

See, this is easy. Kala!

White wine, really? You may need an aspirin in the morning with too much white.

Ass Pro = white.

Ass Pro Kra See, Para Ka LO. F Harry's Toe. –
White wine please. Thank You!

You are doing good now. You are doing very Kala.

13 Big – Mega Low

You want a big beer or a large wine!   Do you want a mega one then? Yes, our slang word for big, mega, comes from the Greek word for big.

Mega low = Big

Mega low Beera Para Ka LO! F Harry's Toe – A big beer please, thank you.

14 Small – Mik Ree

Before you start wondering that this is totally foreign to you and it's all become a Mega low problema (big problem) realise that you have always known Mik Ree is small.

Perhaps if I write it like this Micro(computer chips). Ne, we get our word Micro from Mik Ree, that's small.

Mik R**ee** = small

So we have Meg**a** low beeras and Mik Ree chips. Kala!

15 Chocolate – Soko lata

Come on, this one is easy when you say it out loud it's almost the same sound. Isn't it kala to know that chocolate can be understood nearly everywhere on the planet? Ne?

Soko lata = chocolate

Dax. Mega low Beera ke Soko Lata para ka LO.
Okay, big beer AND chocolate please.

AND is Ke if you want to be really clever. Dax?
Kala.

And = Ke

16 Ice cream – Pagot Oh!

So, chocolate ice cream is Soko Lata Pagot Oh!
Wow, that's very kala of you.

Pagot **o**h = ice cream

17 Another – Enna Allo

As long as you have managed to order one beera and one pagot oh then the rest is easy when you know that Enna **A**llo means another one.

Enna **A**llo = Another

You can of course point to your empty beer glass and plate just to be clear! Dax?

18 Vegetarian - Horto fagos

You want vegetarian ice cream? I've heard of folks asking for such though I never knew there was meat in it. Well, you know our word Horticultural for all things gardening related? It's from Horta for vegetables and salad stuff that Greeks term it.

So if you want to ask for vegetarian meals, say:

Horto fagos? And enjoy your salad.

Horto fagos = vegetarian

Remember to say of course F Harry's Toe after it arrives so they can say Para Ka LO back to you. Kala!

Dax. Ochy problema! Okay, no problem!

---

19 Toilet – Twaletta

It's kind of self explanatory, though after all that beera ke pagot oh you may find this word useful!

Twaletta = toilet

It will interest you to know that, somewhat related, POO Eeena means where is it?

POO Eeena Twaletta? = where is the toilet?

20 Today, Tomorrow, Yesterday – Simmera, Avrio, Heck Tess

Without these words you get pretty much stuck in talking about things and can only ever talk in the present tense, about what you are doing right tora, right now, which may seem pretty obvious to anyone watching.

So. Let's say you are trying to tell the receptionist you want your shower fixed TODAY as your anger is simmering!

Simmera! = Today!

Perhaps you will accept the offer of that tour bus to town tomorrow, or you want to be sure that the bus leaves tomorrow, not today.

Avrio? = Tomorrow?

What if Tess, the chick on reception, is still asking for your passport which you gave to Dimitri yesterday? (we will speak of your passport, Thea Vat**e**erio, later)

Heck Tess! = Yesterday!

When she checks to see they have your Thea Vat**e**erio, she says, 'Dax, Ne! Kala! F Harry's Toe!

21 How much? – Posso Karny?

Dax. You have had your Kra See or Beera or been very kala and had your Nero.

Now you want to know Posso Karny so you can get a Taxi (yes, taxi is taxi, kala isn't it?).

Posso Karny = How much?

Whilst it may be obvious at the end of your taxi journey when you are offering your handful of coins and notes to the driver for them to take whatever it may come to, it is a good idea to ask this as you stand outside of the cab before you commit to the journey as fares can vary.

22 Money, Five to Fifty Euros – Lefta, Pende to Peninder Euros

It's pointless asking how much it is if you have no idea of numbers in Greek, however, asking posso karny will probably give your English accent away and you will be delighted that the answer comes back in English.

This is a useful phrase for visiting shops and petrol stations and also for asking how long you may have to wait.

Euros = Euros

Lepta = Minutes

However, here are the notes denominations, so if you are asked for peninder euros you are into the high numbers and watch out for Eka toh!

Pende = five (the last e is e as in eeg)

Theker = ten (The as in then)

Iko See = twenty

Peninder = fifty

Eka toh! = one hundred

23 Watch out – Pross Secare

Let's hope you never need it but if you do happen to need to shout watch out, think of prosecuted if you don't. Why didn't you tell the guy to get out of the way of the tumbling rock you could see falling down, asks the court prosecutor.

Pross Secare = Watch out!

Perhaps you might need that toilet visit rather urgently after all the Beera, Kra See and Pagot Oh, so this phrase may be useful:

Pross Secare! POO eena Twaletta Para Ka LO! - Watch out! Where is the toilet pleeeeease!

24 Help – Voy Eeeth ia

To add a little drama to the previous phrase, if you really want assistance quickly, add this at the beginning:

Voy Eeeth ia! Pross Secare! POO eena Twaletta! – Help! Watch out! Where is the toilet!

Voy Eeethia = Help

25 Here &There – Ethou & Ecky

Tora, some restaurants might have a twalette right here, or you ask where that Twaletta is because you really need it right tora - and the word Ecki is said with a pointing off into the distance somewhere!

Eth**ou** = Here

Eck**y** = There

26 Stop – Sta matter

What's the matter? What's sta matter do you want me to stop?

When you want your taxi driver to stop because you see your hotel looming up before you, remember to say Sta matter! If you see someone running off with your bag, it may be a good idea to know this too!

Sta matter = stop

Sta Matter! Voy Eeeth ia! Pross Secare! – Stop! Help! Watch Out!

And remember to point in earnest towards the thief running off with your belongings!

27 I've finished – Telios, Have YOU Finished? – Telio Rasee?

By the way, if you want to hang onto your plate as an enthusiastic waiter wants to clear your table, Ocky will serve you well.

Though, as you are so kala at this stuff tora, be aware your waiter will probably say:

Tely or Rasee? And you can say 'Ocky' can't you?
Ne. Kala.

Tely or Rasee = Have you finished (say quickly)

Telios = I've finished

28 Salt – A Lartea

If you fancy a lot of salt, remember

A **Lar**tea = salt

So, if you are not supposed to have much salt for health reasons, or are indeed allergic, how do you think you say, 'no salt please', you can say this, can't you?

Ocky A **Lar**tea Para Ka LO! – No salt please!   Kala! Good!

29 Contains Nuts? Allergic! – Ksiri Carpi? Allerg Ekos!

If you want to ensure that allergic reaction does not happen then, note:

Allerg Ek**o**s = allergic

Remember your intonation in asking questions, your voice must go up at the end else you are telling THEM that this contains nuts! So:

K**s**iri Carp**i** = this is nuts

And

K**s**iri Carp**i?????? =** are there nuts in this?????

By the way, Trell **O**ss is crazy, mad, nuts in the head so hopefully you won't be misunderstood for abusing your waiter!

30 Thief! – Kleff Tess!

Now, if you are unlucky enough to see someone run off with your Val **Ea**tsa (suitcase) though making sure it is not the bell boy at the hotel who is just trying to Voy Eeeth ia, then shout this.

Kl**e**ff T**i**ss! = Thief

So now you can say:

Pross Secare! Voy Eeeth ia, Kleff Tiss! – Watch out! Help! Thief!   And soon you'll be the hero!

31 Are you Okay? - Eeesa kala?

You know that good is Kala, don't you?

Having recovered from your ordeal above, you are likely to be asked:

Ee**ee**sa Kala? = Are you okay?

This is another useful phrase (as they all are) because it is used so very often in greetings. So, having frequented your local hostelry for the return visit, you are likely to be treated as a regular and good friend so will be asked Eeesa Kala? This is because it also means, how are you? To which you of course reply:

Kala! = Good!

Then it is quite easy to return the compliment, isn't it. How would you ask how they are?

Eeesa Kala? = How are you?

If you want to just say, 'you?':

Esies? = You?

32 Call a Doctor - Kal Eese Yatro!

If your holiday is not going well then you may have come off worse in calling your bell boy a thief and now could be in need of a doctor.

Of course, you could just scream out:

Yatro! = Doctor!

I am sure folks will get the message, though if you want them to actually call a doctor for you then you might need to be a bit more specific if there is not the urgency in your voice that the phrase requires, else they might think you are just informing the onlookers of your professional status.

Kalese Yatro! = Call a Doctor!

33 Call Police! – Kalese
Astenomia

If things really have got out of hand now and the hotel staff don't seem to share your viewpoint, it may be in order for you to use this phrase.

Kalese astenomia – Call Police!

Tora, remember you only need Kalese astenomia if you have a mega low problema, ne? Don't go getting the astenomia for non astronomical problems or for mik ree problemas ne? It's only if you really need that voy eeth ia, tora. Dax!

34 I Am Lost – Eho Kathy

Maybe you weren't hurt in the disagreement and decided just to run off and find yourself another hotel, or Xeno tho HeO which literally means a houseful of strangers. You know Xenophobia is fear of strangers? Never mind. It is.

Eho actually means, 'I have' though this is how Greek people term being lost. Just accept it and move on, Dax?

Eho Kathy = I am lost

Though, you might have found a lovely friend called Kathy, so there's always a silver lining.

35 I have lost my passport – Ekassa To Thea Vateerio Mo

Maybe that Kathy wasn't the friend you had hoped and is off on her way with a new identity.

When you speak to the Astenomia this phrase may be useful then.

Ekassa To Thea Vateeri**o** Mo = I have lost my passport. (To as in tok).

Thea Vateerio = Passport.

Though, remember, the very useful Mill Larta Anglik**a** or tell them T**i** Po ta!

If, after that, they don't offer you the necessary voy eeth ia and sympathy, asking you 'Eeesa Kala?' You can ask, Poo Eena Twalette and nip out of the window!

36 Car, Bus, Aeroplane – Aff Tow Kinny, Tow, Leo For Rio, Aero Planno

Kala. Tora, all you need is to get yourself some transportation. Greek folks have mega low words for our mik kree ones sometimes!

How do you want to travel? Perhaps Rio now seems a better option than Greece. Just think, with the right transportation you could be in Rio Avrio! We have some choices here.

Aff Tow Kinny Tow = Car (say quickly)

Leo For **Ri**o = Bus/coach (say quickly)

Aero Planno = Aeroplane

Thank you for reading!

Amazon reviews are really important to future writing projects for independent authors. Please leave a review for me because I would love to hear your thoughts about this book.

If you would like to receive your **FREE** preview of my next book please **email** info@hiprocom.com.

Thank you!

NEW!

Check out our latest book,

'Speak More Greek Badly!' on Amazon!

Printed in Great Britain
by Amazon

34130405R00033